That Which I Touch
Has No Name

JENNIFER K. DICK

That Which I Touch Has No Name

THE **BLACK SPRING**
PRESS GROUP

First published in 2022
An Eyewear Publishing book, The Black Spring Press Group
Grantully Road, Maida Vale, London W9,
United Kingdom

Typeset with graphic design by Edwin Smet
Author photograph Jennifer K Dick
Cover art photo Julien Kauffmann detail of Véronique Arnold's 'Les traces de fil
à travers le temps' (coll. Musée Unterlinden, Colmar, France)

ISBN 978-1-913606-91-6

BLACKSPRINGPRESSGROUP.COM

To my travelling companions
Carole Bouchard (1966-2017)
and Sean Standish

TABLE OF CONTENTS

I/   A CERTAIN PROTOCOL

DEMOLITION

Attempt to become what is probable: I believe
I am not sure to have departed. I refuse to return
to the beginning of that *souvenir et oubli. Souvenir et oubli*
until death becomes dust. It is the return I am after
beginnings. I tell you that I am to forget that I have to
remember to identify what I am. There is a who in the middle
of the crumbling house. I want to be sure to forget.
To go back to the rebuilding. Dust is in our lungs.
There is nothing new in these images moving me
back to recount the forgetting point. To be the erasure
of memory is to begin to begin to be. The sound
of jackhammer, tractor, tank, plane, stone crumbling
in the sand. I am the reverse of my *souvenir-*

oubli Death will never come. It is all, as here, just a matter
of reconstructing under a blue sky in the city of Beirut
where I have never been. I am letting that place I cannot
remember go into that place I will always recall.
This is a process of naming. Let's begin.

COLLECTIF

This

is a protocol
of / for
existence.

Étape 1: inhale.
Étape 2: exhale.
Étape 3: Everything remains 'intraduisible'.

Primo esempio → example 1: Today is a protocol for an existence that is (which is) not mine. Space. A series of right angles, white walls, cog-gear-rush. A regrouping. *Ensemble.* Today is a 'we', enclosed, inked compact company of 10. Come se dice? Dieci? sì? oui? Ceci est "Poets, Inc." Dialogue of diagonals, an assembly of/ for lost funds where 'I' align with 'we'. Coalescence not unlike convalescence. An insider, the body—our body—as an outside in which 'we' is the enclosure. Marbled nymph figurine, 3-pronged trident, sculpted cherubs—these are the gardens rounding the houses of the villages surrounding the paths leading (Jeanne was here, and Charlemagne, too) back to, over, round, into la fabrique. La fabbrica: moulin rouge, the rouge moulin, the red mill wounded. These are the ways a functional protocol of multinational existenz can be conveyed. As the wasp at the skylight thrusts his whole body over and over against the luminous glass, a bike path tunnels through the forest of Compiègne. 2 villages linked like a barbell. A honey stand without its vendor: *Quelle tentation!* 2 ponys, one grey, one white, graze behind an old mansion gate. Stone supports the iron grill. What happened to le manoir? This was once a marbrerie. Inhale. Powder dust white as alabaster penetrates us.

Secondo esempio → example 2: Today is a protocol of existence where uncertainty is the rope surrounding 'us'. Lasso. Laissez-faire. Two continents use the same term but for neither is this related to libidine. Is language within all that 'we' are? An 'our' that is 'are' that is hour howled owl oared criss-crossing. She who promised not to, lied. Ceci est la (sa) (ma) (notre) lingua franca. It's what he said, "Les ruines comme la personne que tu aimes." (A.I.) 'I' believed she was mine. Mined, she was the ruin of 'us'. (Note, not all 'us'es are the same us). Existence is the departure of one body for another. What is begotten in the exchange? No, I know of none who've leapt from the Brooklyn Bridge and survived. To stop cold turkey. To go hog wild. There is a farm between us. A fern. Je suis la chose écartée de l'être, l'être écarté des choses. This could be another portrait 'we' have entitled. Called it « la beauté de l'absence ». In absentia, 'I' signed for 'you'. Who gives one the right for that? Blocks, plaques, stocks, pillars, lungs: l'uomo e straniero à lui-même. Oh, e anche la donna. She inhaled white alabaster marble dust inclining herself towards and towards and then. This, too, was our answer. La prima cosa. Sounds like cause to me, but she hears 'thing' (la chose). Not choice + rule = strategy. Within the enclosure, our departing.

Terzo esempio → example 3: Today is a protocol of connected discontinuities surrounded by a point along a time continuum called 'we', 'us', 'our', 'ensemble'. A co-opted company accompanied by a communitarian commune correlates with... How to calculate the number of rungs on the ladder which will carry 'us' to

that vanishing point? (Insert scene. Look. Out. No—
farther.) Il en faut 2. Due. Deux et. (within none of that
does she hear two, accounting for ladders not rungs.
Meanwhile:) A concomitant number of poets does not
a finite philosophy make. "De penser, lire, écrire ce que
je ne sais pas penser, lire, écrire." I learn to (stop) speak.
I learn to (stop) write. I learn to (stop). Respiro. Pensare
a qualcosa? Quasi-mathematical slivers slither over
the pages, screen. Qui a compté les insectes qui nous
entourent? Font-ils partie de notre 'ensemble' ? Were it
my kingdom, I'd banish the zebra-striped mosquitoes,
grind the gears back into motion, oil the hinges, kick
up a bit of dust. "Funzionare senza..."—à toi de—
fill in the blank, the blanks. The small girl's immense
ballooning halo, she said, "Mistakes of perception".
'I' heard that as 'our' voice. We in the weave of a
weathervane. Iron grate, gate, generators: a protocol
of our physical material is mental (dis)connection.
Unit[(-y) (-ison)]—les interférences, dominate,
dominion: la seconda nota è verde, verdure, that which
perdures, rooted, extending, partiellement occupé
par la chute de l'eau. This protocol is for une île sans
contours. Matrix of metahistories which allow for the
accumulations with the 'us' of 'we' that 'I' eyeing the
falls frees. And what chases after? Point d'isolement et
de réunion. Ponte d'isolamento e comunione. Inhaled.

A FRAME OF

inhabit
inure
lure
lucent
the magic of these syllabic cymbals
clanging against teeth, tongue, jaw
to make what is / isn't
                  isn't / becoming
a hand, pond, drop-off along ocean ridge
to swim out deeper and call forward, undersurface
            where no one hears
                so none that is known knowing can
                sketch or graph into fin,
                      finger, tail, wing
this body's arid language landing arcs round the bay
bluest sapphire, azure
eye or I am drowning / coming up for air

"THE BODY AS MESSAGE"
—Sarah Mangold

Intuit the body asks
                axed
                'relax', she coaxed
strung-out, unwound loophole of imperfection
in the stalemate of someone else's recollection
her herding herself forward and again to go
forth into this bright afternoon unaccompanied
by the whorls of the whims of another's loss

                                                this body

unlatched
absence in
the reassertion of self
space / shame in
a presence of griefs
measured like the height of one child
then the next scratched
out / over wall   :   surface
                                repainted white on white on
as this billboard begins to thrum
this body as tactile in its own
breath(e)
                        she says

                                "just left yourself…"

START-LINGS

"We are beings [un]inhabited by surprise"[(37)]*

> Backlog, backdrift, backdraft of voices out of the chorus, fallen, trembling tremulo of castoff spray sprawling forward into time which has begun to design the definitive end-wall for us to deny that conclusion, define such closure, sit in a row on chaises longues in the late afternoon.

Sunrays reddening.

* Quotes followed by page numbers are all lines or variations of lines in Erin Mouré's *A Frame of the Book*, House of Anansi Press, 1999.

"WHERE THE VANISHED DOUBTED IS PURE CAESURA"[17]

A wounded wilderness
ruin
run over
paved   parchment   placebo
if to construct palisades, le presidio
a palpable sentiment of being rent
i.e. torn—then thrift and trade—with
pulled under
as method for
conveying waterweight

land / sand   shoals
she combed the shellless beaches
for opalesque reminders

a bottle bottles her
up to float
and buoy
and a boy   *ahoy*!   Aloft
listless leftovers on the stained stale mattress
abandoned rooms like pasts like herselves
passersby reflected
'double'   'doubted'   'duplicitous'
sly smile sneer
remembers her in
and then the instant/century
is past

"FEAR IS THE EYE OF MY BEHOLDER" (44)

Cross-path diagonal shift into shadow
the scope of a body
juggernaut
gauged stance,   gait,   gaze
time's gauzy filament lit
spark-blade-muzzle
voice and drum beating against-glass
passersby
                                (motorized)
nighthawks
                                (mobilized)
that which is afloat on the river's surface
crossing underbridge
only the back
head, bloated shirt, a shoe, a foot
bared
boring fear into figment into a fragment
of whose call
it is to make
mould the elbow back into momentum
animate
the still depth of moonpath
a man below
accumulates weight
in our gaze
connects us
to us
to

"...WE ARE NOT CADAVERS"[37]

Still. And yet the rain raining down on us
immobilized, carries cell after cell away:
a complete set of dioxyribonucleic
identification in the acid test of who we
are ought to be tabulation tables of tox
screens of verifications get
what the French call a *bilan* go
down the checklist to confirm and re-
confirm the vital signs seem a
check, a balanced balance is equilibrium
surface tension, pressure under that
membrane we call skin—an organ
remembering us in our pulsing pulsation
a series of 60bpm at 130/80, 140/80—
at what point in the rise alarms raise
hell and highwater to sleep a good
night's waking into day the little death
the o là là and ahhhhh of it sighs
shifted or sifted out into the bustling
day and touch screens register presence
and presences and then, one screen, for an instant
does not feel me there
so that for a flash I am already
absented from myself

"WEIGHT OF" [77]

To touch,   glean,   give
into the fingerprints troubling
the air, an affront afflicted
afterthought
                    honing device
                    homing despite
that which we (I) cannot backtrack to
winnow   :   warlord
drone mosquito hovering overbeach
red bridge   :   tourist trap
shot of   re-collection
                to box up
                seal away,
                overthoughts
In this b&w I am wearing a head scarf
mistaken by a northern tourist
for one of the local Moroccan women
I am dying
faster here
camouflage not
"attentive to doubt or consequence" [77]

THE RUINS OF PAST CIVILIZATIONS–

Neuronets   rocks   replications of
        [urban proximity]
        [planned reminiscences]
        [home]
To be in this place (safe)
or that (safe)   : when
is what is locked away
        [inside(s)]
enough to stave off?
Her hand traces a pattern along stone
leads her from sickbed to market stall
bottled water, banana, yogurt
held down
pressed
to compensate for
the lost, regurgitated sandstorm
grit on windowless windowsill
voiced messages
depart / return
"wherein our particulars vanish
or assume"(90)

FIGURATIVE BLIGHT /

/ our cherished debt
christened green in the ogre-grey
light
collect stones, shells, ants, the carcasses
   of bees, derelict homing predilections
   combing the convex codex for a hived
   intermezzo   /   in stance   /   stead
                 of intermission
   stand   and   re-geolocate
the space   (distance)   place
gold plated between us
like all the "us"es under the domed
structures (scriptures) deciding on
which side "we"   march, attack, land, swoop in,
                 negotiate, obliterate, obfuscate
a small stain appears almost like the word
     "explanation"
         or
     "motive"
on the de-coded documents which have been
99.9% redacted : ███████████████
        This horizontal crossed-out rectangle
could be
       my / your / his / her / their / our
       name/ home / country / ideology / religion / love

NO TITLE

He (33 years old) went missing.

He (19 years old) left his house,

it was missing something.

It suffers from mental disorders.

Knowing the parents of Rabinh

(5 years old) have not returned.

He is wearing a mustard yellow vest,

a dark blue suit or

perhaps what you can see in

this photo. Color? Yes, it's black

and white. It's hard to see

the missing after they've come

back. I named my dog

Amaroun. He went missing

on the day my brother-in-law

lost this blue tie. There is something

about unknown destinations in

his letter. About schizophrenia

running in (and out of) the

family's house—which one of

them hasn't returned yet? A heart

patient, an Alzheimer's clinic will be
held responsible for the weak of
hearing in the absence. Red
messages painted on walls. Wanted
or want-ad posters. He (13 years
old) left his parent's house a
long time ago. What is it about
the i.d. photo taken from be-
hind? I know he is in a
process of departure. This
yellow sting (feel it) isn't
coming back this season. Stamped
on his forehead, suffering in the heat,
call the police should you know
his whereabouts. His body
needs him. What will the girl
he'd struck a date with do? We
are all here at the edge of
the city in the muted
dark awaiting

II/   THE ISLAND

*

Below, the Aegean crashes to shore-shattered bonesplit
stoneshift seasons, perhaps you are right, this full moon's
our cusp tossing us towards winter, but from this cliffside,
shortsleeved in the sweat-sleepless night on night dreaming
another body, another in the gap, winter is merely the
desired melting of ice on lips, licorice clasp of ouzo and
did you say broken? The rusted hull's russet ridge towards
which we steer. You dare not say to deny denial is. Once
love threw herself off the rock's peak. That is what you
wrote. It is one Sapphic myth after another. Do you think
there are small sharks circling on the other side? A drop
off to—*where is this line leading?* There are things—spaces,
blanks, empty mail boxes—that just cannot be taken
seriously (personally) anymore. The waves lap against the
shore, and still the shore is sleep.

*

Did you say hellbent or hellspun? Spurn, spun round
under undercurrents' surfacing, flyflung, dry land's
indescript drought-desert plain of green and beige and
green and beige—And where do we call home? A hand-
on-hip thumbing a ride or catching an aquatic blue
bounty with a twang? (Do you underhear "beauty"?) You
are naught but this blight. Rain on rooftops measuring
humidity, gathering it by the gallons. Leave out the red
nectar for the hummingbirds who'll come back to roost.
Treetop high, you squint and squint trying to catch the
outline of their tiny perch. To pause to punctuate to point.
A direction is signed. A delivery. Carry, to be carried, to
hold now. Can you hear that whisp-whispering? Sound's
surreptitious slippage. Sleepsweat, nightsweats, turning
and returning. We plow, eroding, billowing back and
blacker. This seaseal.

*

You yowl, yearn. The clickity-clack-creak of bodies
turning between dreamspun webbing—healed-hands on
arm, middle-thigh, small of back before the shurusshhhh
knock knock knock of track and train. Riddle-rustled,
opened skeletal branches bracken the ice which holds
us up, an instant's medieval motionlessness before the
buzzing lights, bells whistle again. Skydiving jetstreams
ribbon the atmosphere. Pink dawn breathes into you, waits
edgeless for sea's rising drift. This wavelet, by and bound
backwards into Minerva's caving. This tale you're (re) (and
re) writing, remember? And then you ask who drives the
schools of silvery minnows, black nun-fish, mirrored sea
bass, into the Greek shoreline now that winter has come,
vacating beaches? What terrace firelight recalls post-
midnight, pre-dawn sweat? A sliver of moonlight and
somewhere buzzing.

*

Waves sucked into seagreen breakers breathing taken
over-breadth of (if) only one touch. Glass tides between
us dry splash. This chill cliffside's sliding, sidling by.
Quicker towards our destination. But time waits not for
the fickle, freckled, sucked and sucking back out to sea.
Where is the motored lifeguard, caretaker of parasols
and lazy sunbeds? Who sprinted last out to the edges
of sand and stone and saltwater to get there before the
passing? This *now* you cannot hold in place. This *now*
cannot hold you in place. Midday star falling through
blue sky, white-hot trail: ending indistinguishable from
cloudwisp, crow calls.

*

Battalions and basements, billboards and baseball fields.
We camp. We hold court. You would have tossed
yourself to the wolves, the sharks, the piranhas, but only
minnows abound here, nibbling toes, slipping though
fingernets. What would you have done if a swordfish had
suddenly struck your handheld line off the back of the
paddleboat? We drifted too far out. There were currents
and red nights. There were sunset sailboats and cruise
ships docked for the day puffing diesel fumes along shore
as passengers ferried in and out, in and out. It is like
diving deep down and holding your breath. Bluer than
that. It is Sapphic sapphire. I hand you a stone. I have
rubbed it shiny-smooth with all that is left of me. You
lie against the shore which continues to shape-slip, shift
your body sculpted into sanded forms. What happens
when the wind picks up and blows you out to sea?

*

Slimslipknot light a sliver a sniper I could not sleep, speak,
say to you. This is night nugget, a gold ring, a godless
land or season or memory. Moonlight or lamplight pages
paling. I read your face like braille, with fingertips. Atop the
basilica in Marseilles looking out for the fishermen to return
home, a beacon, a beckoning. Sometimes the to-do list, the
prepackaged, readymade meals, the bus-tram-metro lines
are not enough. She would have reversed time, untossed
her body's overpale form, felt the soles of her feet scuffed,
scraping on the rock's porous edges. You climb higher. I
wade at the base, wondering what is under the otherside,
the exposed seaside softened salted insatiable side where
the seabed drops off and off and—can something hear me
echo if I cry wildly down through the aquatic deep? Depth
of her and here and howl. I close my eyes. I wounded
wonder at this wandering, these drifting icebergs, melting
polar caps for to keeps, in keepsakes, stake this 'til it is kept.
Seasonal middrift, mudslide, making a mess of things. I
have forked path upon path, found my wending way back
to and into and still stilling stiller.

*

This is the stoptime, freezeframe. This is that second
where decision-instinct clash, flight-fate falter stutter.
And then she would leap. Because? She must. You
wrote this over and over. Mines are tales thrust into the
earth where water refuses to respout. This is a desert in
winterflood awaiting our return. I had my back turned
so as not to see that cliff. The sun was blinding even in
December. I cannot tie knots like a sailor. That which
is left adrift finds no tow. Cavernous. This is the dark
luminosity, the shaking touch.

III/ AFTERLIFE

*

When the myth is written you / I become her.
She is.
Dibutade:
She is what has watched departing.
There is a predictability about this.
Her fame is leaving a trace of him.
The lover marked her, she marked the wall with her lover, the wall
was marked a mark was made and was this all simultaneous with
Sappho's leaping? Endings are the part of the women the luminosity
of History refracts.
On an island the ocean erases the trace.
The sand skins the body, a roughness, sculpting away the hardened
surface. It is not a process of emerging, but of erasing. Erasure
makes the form.
But then
there is
Dibutade.
          I / maim
          You / heard
Somehow a 'she' finds herself the 'center' : reversal.
A pronominal name crossed out eventually as presently I might say,
Do you recall the story of Dibutade and you, you would say—*who?*

There is mark making a mark making a mockery of what tracery is. Decor. Divide. A mark can be a boundary enclosing the self enclosed the self departs escapes goes beyond out of bounds of bonds she is standing on the threshold where the women stand on the threshold while the departures are happening farther beyond their gaze and Sappho leaps, decisive, but who sees her seeing her step forward beyond the last mark fragmenting into a crack in her story? I meant to tell you about Dibutade. I did not mean to conflate woma(e)n.

As in
Dibutade = Echo = Sappho = me/you/us/I/they
Di
But
Ade
is an echo:

> "In Classical Antiquity, one of the most pervasive legends of the origin of drawing and of painting describes the tracing of the outline of someone's shadow, thrown onto a surface either by candlelight or by natural sunlight (sciagraphy). Pliny the Elder

is beauty reflected
from hiding

> in his *Natural History* attributes not only the origin of drawing to this method, but also the origin of clay modeling.

shadowform by the reedy pond
Dibutade-echo only a silence,

> Pliny tells the story of a potter of Sicyon in
> Corinth, named Butades (in French 'Dibutade'),
> who invented clay modeling through the actions
> of his daughter. Butade's daughter, who possesses
> no independent name in the story, but who is
> often referred to as the 'Maid of Corinth', traces
> an outline on a wall of the shadow of her lover's
> face cast by the light of a lamp.

only the repetition of other, of him.
Her body leans outward into the night into the space into the moments of....
Elsewhere, Sappho leaps.

Her fame is not her own fame but it is that of the body lost to her.

> Her lover is soon to leave, and the profile will
> provide her with memory of him." — *Encounters
> with the Other,* Martin Calder

A reversal is in the clay of the father, the hands, the potter making the form
rise out of the earth, calling it back.

Butade's daughter possesses no independent name.
She is not in the story.
She is not.

       History   has erased
      her mark

              is him marked

onto the wall is he the mark left is she in the traces part of the line of
him embodied in the line of that charcoal not blown away on a sandy fall
afternoon not dispersing over time as Sappho perhaps is leaping also into the
void

                            Until it is / and then it is the men
The father
Reforming from the wet earth the body of the lost:
Does he call him back for her?
Does he watch her pine away in the absence of him?
What does she leave of herself if not the mark of the man on her?
The myth is called the myth of Dibutade. But this is not her name.
She has no name at all.

In Pliny's *Historia Naturalis* the history of painting consumes him.
Chapter 35 emerges.
It tells us that "when the girl's father discovers this, the first drawing,
he molded the form in clay and fired it in his kiln."
Victor Burgin tells us that "In a letter of 1843 to Mary Russell, Elizabeth Barrett
writes, 'I long to have [...] a memorial of every being dear to me in the world[...]'"
Every being memorialized in the line, the trace the mark marked name the named
naming of the other and the self, does the self suffer in its own observation?
In its own invisibility?
Go ask Dibutade.

She is only a part of a myth, an illusion, a recollection of
a line traced onto the wall.
One night, a lover left for a war and never came back.
This is an original story.

//

There is something about departures in the naming of Dibutade.
There is something that sounds stuck in the mud.
Or (e)merging.
She stands on the threshold by the wall that is no longer blank.

What is in a name?

A language traced onto her through her, embroidered back into him.
What can we touch when our fingers rise to the tension of the white
smudged.

I suppose, perhaps, we will hear her, hearing him hearing her heard or heralding a shift as in there came a trembling not yet measurable by contemporary implements that accounts for far-later-to-be-understood tectonic plate shifts in an atmosphere of the unknowing universes of a space that is as proximate as one breath puffed out towards another in a Siberian winter far off from the cascading cliffs of Sappho or the door where Dibutade is waiting still in the reddening sunset of her own departure or her own voicing, of her now put your ear to the door the passage of time to the space in which a foot lifts and moves, re-articulated into the pages of some passing.

Dibutade

Leans out into the night, listening. Turns back, she is turned back inside, like an item of clothing inside out with her inside is, she, is she in the trace, in the house, in the wall in the walls of the house emptied of him in she is within the shaken line, the tracing, his body resculpted into three dimensions by her father accentuating the departed absence of being in movement in dialogue by the line on the wall inside the house where a woman without a name recalled as the origin of something like art is asking is a part apart of the asking is there a self in the mark-making. Wouldn't you like to know. Her. Name. Voice.

Dibutade is

at a loss, she lets herself go out into the ether, into the
air, into the specter of where he might have gone

shadowform scratched into stone wall, into her skin, his
silhouette emerges in the night, calling to her

Tracings intact. Voyages. The mouthfeel of the words of places she wonders whether he travels to. Humboldt writes of fallow orange trees, unrooting. What does not flourish in the open air?

Beside her, here. Her hearing intact as she fingers the tracings left of him on the wall.

Wondering / Wanderlust

What flourishes from the 37th to 40th degree of latitude:
Chamaerops
date-trees
sugar-cane
the banana

When in the kingdom of Valencia…

She browses, opaque, opacity,
Recognize: the hard to understand, lack of the lucid.
Pages and pages burning in the backdrop.
She coats her hands, her face with the blackened remains.
She draws his figure on stone, over and over, as if to lure him back.

That which is lurid. That which is luminescent. That which is languishing,
limpid, longing.
The L of
The L of
The L
Lamppost light lingers over lunarscape pavement. Pacing. Palimpsest.
His body over. Her beginnings over. And over again.

To compare the dust and ash to what remains. He is her Pompeii.
He is Pompeii in her. She stares through the Vesuvian night cratering her
as if in dream lifted to alight atop the arc: indecent absence.

What in the naming of farewell implies forlorn?

No one can tell her she did not know.

War, after all, in the warp and weft,
in the wanderlonging lingering,
in her transformation.

          Candle and oil lamp in the shuttered dark,
          opening,

                 a ray of sun, just now, pierces her.

He

        is ensnared, skinned

                    torse nue
                    a whisper:

that which is cut from the cloth
that which is severed from the body
that which is slivered by wind and stone

He who

nightflight, dayhowl hurl and lit

ailes repliées
ailes refoulées
a cough, a light

He passes through the tunneled tubular vision
spotdarklight mimeographed telescopic groping

is netted, nettles, stung and singing
through the singed grout appearing

rapt
disheveled
momentous

vide de l'abîme entre nous
de le toucher, de l'atteindre
… de ces vignes, forêts, sacs poubelles

voiced embodiment of the fantomatic decline:
His angular descent.
No. Hear, angular descent. No. Here. He is, heralded.

Labor   Labyrinth   Landlocked

        Lathe   Leaden

Levee   Level   Ligament

        Limonite   Litmus

Lobule   Longitude   Lowering

        Loquacious   Lucent

Luminary   Lupine   Lymphoid

                         Lyric

Dibutade is

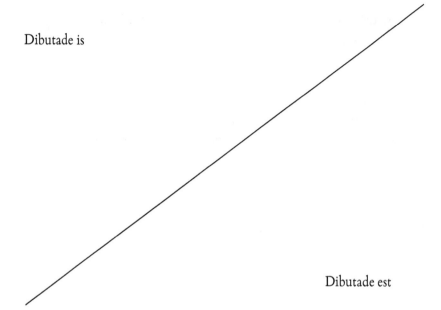

Dibutade est

désorientée, elle le poursuit dans l'éther, dans l'air, dans
le spectre des lieux possibles où le retrouver

L'empreinte de l'ombre gravée dans la pierre murale, dans
sa peau, sa silhouette émerge dans la nuit, l'appelant.

Calques intacts. Voyages. La sensation dans la bouche des mots d'endroits elle se demande s'il y voyage. Humboldt écrit sur des orangers qui ne poussent point. Déracination. Qu'est ce qui ne s'épanouit guère en plein air ?

A côté d'elle, ici. Son ouïe intacte elle suit avec ses doigts les traces qu'il laisse sur le mur.

Voyance / Voyageur

Ce qui végète du 37ème au 40ème degré de latitude :
Chamaerops humilis
Dattier
Canne à sucre
Le bananier

Une fois au royaume de Valencia…

Elle feuillette, opaque, opacité,
Reconnaître : ce qui est difficile de comprendre, le manque de lucidité.
Des pages et des pages brûlent en arrière-plan.
Elle couvre ses mains, son visage des vestiges noircis.
Elle dessine sa forme sur la pierre, encore et encore, comme si elle pouvait provoquer son retour.

Ce qui est vif. Ce qui est vu. Ce qui est vivant, virevoltant, vadrouillant.
Le V de
Le V de
Le V
Volumineuse vidange dans le Viaduc des Arts. Arabesques couvertes d'arcs
d'anciens chemins d'eau. Vitesse. Palimpseste. Son corps par-dessus. Ses
débuts par-dessus. Et encore déçue.

Comparant la poussière et les cendres à ce qui reste. Il est son Pompéi.
Il est Pompéi en elle.
Elle perce du regard la nuit Vésuvienne qui la berce comme dans un rêve
soulevé pour se poser sur l'arc : l'absence indécente.

Qu'y a-t-il dans l'évocation d'adieu qui implique le chagrin ?

Personne ne peut lui dire qu'elle ne savait pas.

La guerre, après tout, dans la chaîne et trame,
dans l'errance désirée et durable,
dans sa transformation.

       Chandelle et lampe à huile dans l'obscurité à volets clos,
       ouverture,
              un rayon de soleil la perçant à l'instant.

Il

     est pris au piège, écorché

           shirtless
           chuchotement:

ce qui est fait de la même étoffe
ce qui est coupé du corps
ce qui est tailladé par le vent et la pierre

Lui qui

Voldenuit, hurlementdujour lancé et allumé

refolded wings
repressed wings
une toux, une lumière

Il traverse la vision tunnel tubulaire
Pointd'ombrelumière ronéotypé tripotage téléscopique

est pris au filet, orties, piqué et chantant
à travers l'enduit de joint brûlé qui apparait

captivé
débraillé
capital

The emptiness of the abyss between us
To touch, to reach
… from these vines, forests, trash bags

incarnation articulée à vive voix du déclin fantomatique :
Sa chute angulaire. Non. Entendez : chute angulaire. Non. Ici.
Il est, proclamé—

Vacante   Vacarme   Vagabonde

      Validité   Valse

Vaporeuse   Vaste   Végétatif

      Veille   Veinosité   Verbiage

Verdissement   Vermiculaire   Vestale

      Vexant/Vexation/Vexatoire   Vidéographe

Votif   Vouer   Vrille

                  Vu(e)(s)

Circulaire

/

Tourbillon

notre rêve n'est pas ivre de…

près de lui, elle

      se recule

      recourbant

      recluse — renfermée — éloigne-toi de

                  lui / elle
                  part

              aux montagnes
                lointaines
              ciel rouge
              chapeau en paille

        il fait chaud l'après-midi donc
        elle ne prend la fuite que la nuit
        dans le noir elle
            s'abandonne

Ainsi
ou ensuite
on va à sa poursuite cherchant un signe

    elle n'avait pas laissé de message

    devant le portail qui s'ouvre au village

    [pas de mot pour eux / nous / les habitants / son père / son amant]

Elle n'était pas si belle, Dibutade, pas si
riche ni douée d'une pensée particulière—mais quand même
on se souvient de la trace

sa trace

de lui

qu'elle

a laissé sur un mur

                      le mur intérieur
                      loin du regard

cette trace

                      n'est pour elle
                      pour qu'elle
                      se souvienne
                      de cet homme
                      lui, qui n'est
                      qu'à elle

toute seule

Mais on entre
(J'entre)

dans la maison :
              anthropologue
              archéologue
              socio-culturel historien d'art de ce qui reste de…

et nos doigts touchent
retouchant la courbe du signe laissé
par (pour) son amant (amour)

Est-ce que cela, le sens du vide intérieur ?   Une ligne
                                                            un chemin
                                                            une voie vers

(pas vers)

la trace qui mène,
                  ramène à

                                    Dibutade

                                                          Devient

Devenir

Une trace retraçant une histoire d'un corps

un art

oublié par la (sa) (notre) mémoire

Je m'y penche

Ailleurs, Sappho se lance dans la mer

Dibutade s'éclipse de l'histoire

Comme son amant

J'entends quelque chose près de la fenêtre

De la maison abandonnée

Et puis je pense à lui, à elle

notre solitude à deux

(et deux mille)

Traversée par le temps

(entre)

(nous)

(voie) (voix) (verre)

de sa transparence

Une ligne émerge

et là, toute l'Histoire de l'Art

retisse, renoue, renouvelle, recommence, renonce, réinvente, se remémore de
　　　　　　　　　　　　　　　　　　　　　　　　et alors, encore,
　　　　　　　　　　　　　　　　　　　　　　　　Dibutade

Qui pense parfois que l'amour l'a passée
la dépasse

dans le code des choses
son départ

　　　　A crescent is a sparrow is a startling lineage

　　　　Dibutade / Sappho
　　　　You / Me
　　　　Son père / Son amant

　　　　The raven in the window = a message

　　　　if she could peel open / s'enroule

　　　　　　　　　　　　　　sleight of hand
　　　　　　　　　　　　　　pomegranate
　　　　　　　　　　　　　　seed a series
　　　　　　　　　　　　　　of very small
　　　　　　　　　　　　　　lines in the verbiage
　　　　　　　　　　　　　　she snatches at
　　　　　　　　　　　　　　etches

the underside of a singularity

to bind her
   blind

La contrainte
l'aveugle
l'efface
l'adore
l'oublie

que
ce que
Dibutade est

Vu(e)(s)

IV/   CONVEXITY

"SIMULACRA QUENCHED A BITTER NERVE."[(91)]

The day morose.   The body
in splinters.   The mind arcs
out : a lightningbolt snapped
against metal,   sparks
night   day   night   day
rain
            dream of a pool wading
through bright blue chlorine
note the lamp plugged into
wallsocket underwater fear
the sharp electric thrumm
push   on   into
            the day dawn drawn noon
cavelike   yaw of wind
winnowing leaves from trees. A saw,
a motorbike, a voice. The city de-
emerges from its cocoon. Candlewax
melting over limestone :
re-coded messages left over
trinkets, cameras, nightvision goggles
engines endlines ears flickering globe
turning towards December : winter's
"Spectral anguish."[(91)]

WHEREWITHAL

"where once no life was possible
a true life"[34]
   was sought to concoct a "stake in" [34]
                        settle round bee's nest
hive-hum doctoring directionality
      from equation's equanimity
the infinities out of *that* infinity
      Cantor's paradox
for one mind, numbers out of time
  slipshorn, straddled between being
and
  the day's halfworn heels carrying
the body to its next destination
  a sidestepped stumble-screech
of ornamental owl perched on windsill
to make nightlife flee
   the way
   the wear
   the wanton
                 in the design (signation) of what is
                                    (or is not)

DESI[RED]

Hand rakes through ruddy blonde hair
she speaks of her
and her
how no one heard the same
longing—yet the time spent
close
in quarters
quarters her, rent wet body destined
to open   if / to
                    while the story, told, is like a small object—
                    knickknack knockoff souvenir spent
                    —collected, settled in the dark of the *terrasse*
                    table between us
as here my own knowing (of) what
longing and love are rekindled
for an instant's flicker
          a wave
          a bat
          a crowd of passersby   Our voices
hear how the sharp blade is honed.

WE ARE EACH MOMENT SHOCKED

The Virgin River, a sluice-sliver rush
between desert and stone, canyon and mountain,
sun rising to burn us bright through
the red hole hallowed
in the omniscient silence, lean
      over-ridge
be honest

                        that what can be seen
                        sought
                        rain, stone, meteor
is still crashing   collapses
over and over
      in some universe, time
      inversed
      upside-down green
      quay-like cratered
the storytelling national guard stepping back
      and closer still
her perch as (un) (in) certain for her as my eye
eyes the skid of rock
formations between the lyre
and sky
your song of my / our / their / her lives (selves)
collapsing inwards
      then a breath, deeper,
      her foot carries her forward
      nettles, brush, cacti catch to
      pierce us along the path drawing away

POPULAR MECHANICS

"Je cherche tout simplement à vous abolir
My precious consequence"[46]

the boxed thing
is what I said in the blank
my precious consequence
abolition of our narrative
storylines un-twine
numeric divisions
lack something of the spectacular
name-in-lights neon
a worm wends his body round our garden
paths overgrow their usefulness

       to carry

       an action

       akin to tides

measure erosion
our   abolition / oblivion
among the stacks a sense of conversion
from the flesh / body to plastic
the utility being | a factor | of us

SENT – RECEIVED

Many graces are
slipped that she may bore or
bald, greasy—a foehn of loss, my
palm-frond an Easter given to laughter.
Understand, what is stated is not my
fortuned favorite bland but taste
of these pages.
Withdraw into your corner,
regroup to spit out the blood
of this frail over-paddling against-
current.
Where one told the other a lie, a
gilded-grey cityscape signalled numerology
wherein a she counts up to zero. Count back
down again: our joy sheds meaning, glimmer
silvery.
The murderer's mercurial mirror is a pelican
of loosened lies. Where are, who are,
you/I/we/she/they? A sore grace, a scent of
skinned doves, lovers loosened into
the night. Wait by that door until you hear
the hinges creak.
"List as boats do / going under"[62]
The glories of the ancient world plundered,
ground to dust in the flash of an aria. Won't you
come back, sing to me?
What's slumber to a king alone
beside a darkened swarm of awaiting suitors?
Take her by her hive. Plot the original crime along
cracked alcoves, between tea services on settees.
Pluck with excited opalesque fingertips
each nail off one by one. Scales passed, pliers

let go. Don't screen for softness
when sharpening the bone.

THERE IS SOMETHING ABOUT

the permanent impermanence
Berrigan's "and I am all of them!"
or "when will I die? I will
never die" the dash
of swallow, pigeon's dovecoo
carrying the virus in its
downy undercarriage: snuggle close
to whisper secreted longings
light lengthening towards
end-of-days
orange – red: ochre
words sought out like lovers
groped in the night.

MICROCOSMS

A crescent is a sparrow is a startling
Albino raven in the windowsill's message
Peeled her open to a series of very small words
Contained in the cavity of her bosom, in the ribcaged thoracic concavity
Of loss, or lost losses: codes akin to relocation memorialized in her
Tattooed surface: skin hearing the nothingness of happenstance shadowscapes
Snow in the rhyme and list, the underhaul, the *heave-ho!*
Grappling hook sunk deep into whaleflesh, bone-corseted labial need
Tinny singularity an event horizon she can almost perceive
Crescent-bound to blind / bind her
As if love Skyped in just then to say "Hello!"
Catcall through tubular hollows
L'étage (étagère) suivant(e): blocage / brouillage of man-tree-oaken aged
Timeless concentric sound of her aspiration: the articulation of a curve
A forested frequency: the pitch of his gesture
Call-cornered-cradled-whimpering-grudge she sludges through
A real trooper, that gal, hurdling happenstance in the lost hopeful
Last leg of the noted race whitewashed windowledge
A linguistic trellis is a logarithmic lockbox
Noting safety in the singed wing's arced descent
A boulder is a notebook, a ringed beginning: gilded

IN WAR

Trees list in wind
a dog howls
cats lick paws clean, yawn
in sunpools
roaches race undercounter
towards coveted crumbs
scarcity sensed in impatience
in the absence of
clean running water, electricity
a static hum
no longer planes plying tourists
with heated destinations, sweaty incompre-
hension, the discomfort of that foreign
bed
        she turns in the night
        to face
        the house she loved
        its walls
        agape
        maw exposed to snippets
        of sniper-fire
each morning awaits
some attenuated
conclusion
        takes up her books
        traverses solitary lanes
        to the surprise of mothers
        a game of pretending
        normality back into place:
simple as restoring the cracked
statue's severed head
to its roost. A process
of redefinition

"DOES CORPORALITY BEREAVE?"(100)

The narrative
not-hers, of knots heard
in the woodpecker's knock
8,803 miles above sea level
Imperial Point's gaze grasping at air
in/exhale the grand
gasp of cavernous canyon
abovesea red green grey stone
into which fog pools
mystical Merlinesque mask
above abandoned streams winnowing
fissures through stonescapes
whiteout winterevenings a boarded fence
red mudslide along the Vermillion Cliffs
one after another
natural
disasters seemed a sign
to keep at bay
visitors
up to the now-crepuscular granite
and sandstone, limestone and calcite
shards of flint, quartz, dolomite
scrape hand, knee, elbow, her entire
body raw
with the desire
for loss

PLACE :

Is a
dis-place-meant
        in the means of

location
      A singular

                 number of years
                 spent

                 To account for
                 locale: isn't it
      [to opt out
        or into:]   immeasurable

                 divisions?

That which is rent from one

In this movement

separrejeuvenation
                 a cultural-linguistic
                 promise
                 name   home
                 plane   schlepped car
                 shipped to walk
                 stop
                      —and then
locate the "exile" in "reconciliation"
of frontiers and calculable numbers
of words available in each of her tongues
un-cross-stitched from what one was / is

the average
trans-

       stamp thumped on a block of papers
       declares her   Hearing
                            is in
           a quieter tone: this
      place of all echoes
              the palimpsestic
              singular

AXIOM OF CHOICE

On gravitas, spheres, and other mobilized celestial beings

Pythagore et l'école de Crotone vers 530 av. J.C.
« la Terre est sphérique »
parce que « la sphère est la plus belle de toutes les figures solides. »
Aristote (IVème siècle av J.C.) écrit
Traité du ciel.
Il observe la forme circulaire de l'ombre projetée par la Terre
sur la surface de la Lune lors des éclipses de Lune.
Aristote voyage, et il remarque « qu'un voyageur se déplace du Nord
vers le Sud et voit
que certaines constellations disparaissent
tandis que de nouvelles s'élèvent.»
Enfin, dit-il, la Terre doit être sphérique
pour des raisons de
symétrie et d'équilibre.

Moi aussi, je voyage du Nord au Sud. Le ciel se transforme non
pas parce que je ne vois plus les mêmes constellations, mais parce
que je m'éloigne de la lumière de Paris. À Paris et à Mulhouse, les
deux villes où je réside, les lampadaires ont été installés de façon
préméditée. Ils ont été attachés à la façade des immeubles, implantés
aux points équidistants pour que la lumière se projette vers le sol et
illumine les chemins et les rues pour les piétons. Des lampadaires
ont été installés par une personne embauchée par l'adjoint au maire,
un adjoint qui a dicté un budget. Il a esquissé d'une manière précise
un plan pour mettre des lumières partout dans la ville. Souvent,
on entend les citoyens de Paris et de Mulhouse dirent que l'adjoint
au maire doit avoir un ami qui travaille dans la fabrication des
lampadaires. Le nombre et le volume et la luminosité des lampadaires
se multiplient et se multiplient et se multiplient.

Ainsi, le Ciel s'éloigne. On ne constate pas l'ombre de la Terre sur la Lune. Les pointes blanches qui forment des constellations s'effacent, sont abandonnées aux regards des corps célestes. De nos jours, les étoiles vivent leur existence bien au-delà des regards des citoyens de Paris et de Mulhouse qui se promènent sous les couvercles de lumières des lampadaires. On dit que les lampadaires sont là pour la sécurité de tous. Ils nous protègent en nous enfermant sous des demi-sphères de lumière, cocons d'illumination. De tels arcs de luminosité forment une aveuglante barrière aux étoiles célestes. S'il vivait de nos jours, Aristote n'aurait pas eu les repères nécessaires pour écrire son *traité*. Il serait rentré tranquillement du bar du coin sous la caresse des LED, ne pensant qu'à la terre et au béton sous ses pieds. Peut-être qu'il aurait composé un traité bien plus terrestre. Il aurait contemplé les insectes attirés par la lumière des lampadaires. Ou pire. Imagine : Aristote, qui rentre bien tranquille sous la douce lumière des lampadaires et, au lieu de se mettre au travail, décide d'opter pour le lit et ses rêves ?

Mais Aristote marchait dans le noir sous les sphères de l'univers en contemplant leurs mouvements. Je marche dans le noir à Piane et vois le ciel d'Aristote. Nos regards se croisent un instant.

Enfin, me dit-il, la Terre doit être sphérique
pour des raisons de
symétrie et d'équilibre.

L'œuvre de Ptolémée sera l'aboutissement des réflexions d'Aristote sur la sphéricité de la Terre. Elle sera l'Omega. I decide to sketch him back into Aristotle's visions of an idealized equilibrium. Standing mid-field in the night near the Roman ruins of the stockroom staring up into the stars shooting across the sky through and against time he looks into this bowled expanse of universe projecting itself over him and the expanse of time between us evaporates. A line is drawn by our gaze. The difference of two spheres culminates in a paradox, for "a pea can be chopped up and reassembled into the

Sun". For one, the world is of symmetry and balance. For another it is an infinite set of balls, one inside the other, like Russian dolls. For a third, we become Polar Coordinates on a plane extending over centuries. I am the point (P) looking up and back which the ray extending from the fixed pole or point of Origin (O) from where Ptolemy stands looking up and forward reaches.

Je sais que Ptolémée (à Alexandrie, en Égypte) vivait et regardait et étudiait le cosmos à 2024.461837 KM d'où je suis actuellement (ici à Piane di Bronzo, en Italie), et qu'on a un écart d'environ 1916 et 1848 années entre nos vies si on calcule cela à partir de l'an 2016 et les années de sa vie (100-168 après JC) et que la latitude et longitude du point à mi-distance entre nous deux est 37°08'30" N et 021° 34' 53" E. De plus l'azimut entre nous est 312°51'41.70" et l'azimut inversé est 121° 57' 30.57". Mais alors, si on regardait la même étoile depuis nos points de vue rétrospectifs, comment mesurer l'espace-temps qui nous sépare? Combien de temps faut-il pour que nos regards se croisent, se rencontrent, se retrouvent ensemble à la surface d'une étoile filante?

Delaunay écrit : « L'œil est notre sens le plus élevé, celui qui communique le plus étroitement avec notre cerveau. »

Hold yourself tight against gravitational shift and pull. Lasso and lassoing. Freestyle.

We are the subsets of history in decomposition, reconfiguration. Dépiècés. Departure as in expedition as in exploration of the spheres, perfection of the absolute circle. Line turning infinitely around and into itself. Ouroboros.

À tout moment Ptolémée pouvait établir les positions des cinq planètes visibles
à l'œil nu : du Soleil et de la Lune.
Ptolémée se basait sur ses modèles géométriques

Modèles composés de cercles
Cercles ensuite convertis en tables
Ensuite traduites et ré-traduites, illustrées, enluminées,
Enfin imprimées
La syntaxe mathématique
L'Almagest

Later, taking into account the third dimension like a third eye,
it would be shown that one could obtain infinite orbs from one.
Using the Banach-Tarski paradox, it is possible to obtain k copies
of a ball in the Euclidean n-space from one, for any integers $n \geq 3$
and $k \geq 1$, i.e. a ball can be cut into k pieces so that each of them is
equidecomposable to a ball of the same size as the original... These
results then extend to the unit ball deprived of the origin.

Aristotle believed there is no effect or motion without cause.

Conversely, light bodies such as the element fire, move by their
nature upward toward the inner surface of the sphere of the Moon.

For Newton, this would have to do with force being.

Is planetary gravitas proportional to my (Aristotle's) (Ptolemy's)
longing to take to the road?
Witness the shift of shadow on lunar planes, the way some but not
all constellations evaporate into the dark.
Sight the circumpolar star, that which cannot vanish.
Catalogue the characteristics of the flawed orb, the failure to sketch
the circle freehand.
How the self fractals, shattered, fractals again.
The secretion of psychic tendency: to sketch the universe based on
the floating gods.
I am uplifted and sleep in the cobalt air.

ASSAY

"Assay": First known use: 14th century.

1. archaic: Trial. Attempt.

2. : examination and determination as to characteristics (as weight, measure, or quality)

3. : analysis (as of an ore or drug) to determine the presence, absence, or quantity of one or more components; *also*: a test used in this analysis

4. : a substance to be assayed; *also* : the tabulated result of assaying

(*Merriam-Webster* online, 2016)

Within the unencounterable others we read is another self we take into ourselves. The resulting poetry is dialogic, even as it emerges like a vector seemingly from a singular point/voice. We are all part of a conversation. In the case of *That Which I Touch Has No Name*, the conversation is as much one that is with other poets and their poetry, as with myself, as with readers. Initially, what informs this work is how I am reading through visual and textual fields of others as if they were fuzzy reflections of the self in the (dis)(re)connectives. Movement. Inertia. The thought. The felt. I took and unhinged lines from Erin Mouré's *A Frame of the Book* (House of Anansi Press, Canada, 1999) from June 2015 to June 2017 in an uncharted attempt to unearth something that has to do with the equilibrium between the space of that blank page and (my/a/our/no)self in the urban heart—that crashing disturbance of the Paris home—or that is in the quasi-pastoral landscape residing on 3 borders when I find myself in Mulhouse (an echo of my Iowa roots: how did I return to such silence? And yet, what are those mountain peaks—les Vosges, the Black Forest—doing here if this town echoes that one back on the plains of the United States?).

Do these statements have anything to do with the poems I've been writing? Those I am presenting here? Perhaps. Perhaps not. I cannot quite pin down all of that white (both in and outside me), but something keeps at me, an inking, a verbal construction akin to emerging. These poems, this book is thus a project that has gnawed away the thick resilient *Frame* of Mouré's. It is conceivably asking: What structures, holds up, contains, leaks out of our pages, our self(v̨es)? The singularity of plural experience, and the plurality of singular experience infuse and perchance in turn are infused by these pages. Things are gathered(ing) here: Memory creation.

What is re-collected sometimes surprises me. Thus these poems interrogate the space of that which may be language but which is not felt by the body or the mind, that is like an inkling of emerging vocabularies, linguistic minefields of the forgotten, written over, re-emergent or buried tongue felt dividing, estranging, subjugating the space of emergence. Parallel: frame of the fading mirror reflection of a self. Insert here: plus—as in, plus politics, plus travel, plus identity papers, plus religion, plus news reports, plus disguises and masks, plus science and fantasy, plus the messiness of desire, plus autobiography after a period of dementia. Loss holding the thing relocated after a period of not realizing it was missing. Some men came out onto the streets and shot a bunch of people in Paris. This had never happened here before. Many poems were written after that moment. And yet, what do they have to do with that instant in time? The way one action ricochets and recalls another, the Grand Canyon, a trip to Morocco, the body/time/language in movement.

Perhaps what "informs" my writing is a lot of dis-information.

NOTES & CREDITS

BIBLIOGRAPHICAL REFERENCES:

Many of the poems and titles in section I & IV use quotations, or variations on lines from Erin Mouré's *A Frame of the Book*, House of Anansi Press, 1999. Her original page numbers are indicated in grey typescript in this book. Note on the variations: page 9: I added "un" to her original which reads "We are beings inhabited by surprise". Page 10: Mouré's original reads "where the vanished double is pure caesura". Page 13: I compacted language from 4 lines by Mouré to make this closing line.

"Demolition" and "No Title" as well as numerous elements in the poems on pp 7-15 emerged following visits to the *Mer Méditerranée (Mediterranean Sea)* exhibition by Rabih Mroué, Kunsthalle Mulhouse Centre d'Art Contemporain, Mulhouse, France, Sept 17th-Nov 15th 2015. "No Title" was highly informed by his video installation piece "Noiseless".

Collectif: AI= Andrea Inglese; poem started at Le Moulin Rouge, Verberie, France.

Ted Berrigan references in "There is Something About" are from his poem *Red Shift*.

Part III: quotation 1: *Encounters with the Other: A Journey to the Limits of Language Through Works by Rousseau, Defoe, Prévost and Graffigny* Martin Calder (Rodolpi, 2003) quotation 2: Victor Burgen re-quotes this letter from 1843 leaving out the married names of both women. The original quote is published in Raymond, Meredith B., and Mary Rose Sullivan, eds. 1983. *The letters of Elizabeth Barrett Browning to Mary Russell Mitford, 1836–1854*. 3 vols. Vol. 3. Waco, Texas: Armstrong Browning Library of Baylor University.

"Axiom of choice": document-based poetry project quoting from Wiki documents on the Banach-Tarski Paradox, Aristotle, and Pythagoras, from various sources on Ptolemy, and geological specialty sites for the calculations. The Robert Delaunay quote is from *Du cubisme à l'art abstrait*, Paris, S.E.V.P.E.N. 1957, p. 146. Citation taken from https://www.cairn.info/revue-chimeres-2006-2-page-49.htm#no1.

POEM ACKNOWLEDGEMENTS:
I would like to thank the following magazine, anthology, artbook and chapbook publishers for including this work in earlier versions:

Estepa Editions, France and Kate Van Houten for *No Title* which appeared as a single fold-out poem chapbook in November 2015, and for the seven poems in section II called "The Island" which appeared as *Conversion* (2014 artbook edition of 50 handmade boxes containing the 7 poems each as a folio page on ancient Italian paper printed with ink and watercolors by Kate Van Houton).

Angel House Press, Canada, for their lovely chapbook version of *Afterlife* which appeared in June 2017.

The transnational anthology edited by Jane Nakagawa called *women : poetry : migration* (Theenk Books, New York/USA, 2017) in which the poems "Place :", "Simulacra quenched a bitter nerve", "Weight of", "The ruins of past civilizations" and "Figurative Blight" as well as a condensed version of the craft essay "Assay" appeared.

Benway series *foglio 9*, in which an excerpt from "Collectif" appeared in October 2014 in English and Italian and *Le Moulin*, a 28-minute long film by Gilles Weinzaepflan, 2013, in which I read an extract from "Collectif".

Parentheses: thanks to Ed Smallfield and readers at Collage-Barcelona for including "Demolition" and "Fear is the Eye of My Beholder" in their first issue (Barcelona, spring 2017)."

Tears in the Fence: thanks to David Caddy and Westrow Cooper for including "Microcosms" and "There is something about" in issue 64 (Dorset, UK, Sept 2016).

I would also like to thank the visual artists Véronique Arnold and Miranda Gavin along with dancer Olivier Gabrys for inspiring 'Afterlife' and the collaborative project and performance *Traces de son amant qui s'en va* that took place at the Musée des Beaux Arts in Mulhouse on May 31, 2013.

Gracious thanks also to Virginie Poitrasson, Eléna Rivera, Sue Chenette, George Vance, Lisa Pasold, Emmanuèle Jawad, Martine Fade, Enrico Monti, Tania Collani and Déborah Heissler for their attentive readings and advice about this book, especially on my French and Italian writing. Thanks also to Black Spring Press Group editors and readers for their selection for publication and careful layout of this collection.

A final shout out goes to *le Moulin Collectif I*—the group of Italian and French poets with whom I spent time at Le Moulin Rouge in Verberie by Compiègne in France in the summer of 2014 writing, translating, filming and revising the poem "Collectif", including Gilles Weinzaepflen, Laurent Grisel, Anne Kawala, Marc Perrin, Michaël Batalla, Mariangela Guatteri, Renata Morresi, Alessandra Cava, Andrea Inglese, and visual artist Florence Manlik. *Collectif II: Documenta/Spaghetti Western* with four of these same authors took place in summer 2016 in Tuscania, Italy and led to this book's closing poem.

CPSIA information can be obtained
at www.ICGtesting.com
Printed in the USA
BVHW080751130222
628727BV00001B/53